Lent with Sister Vassa

Reflections for Every Day of Lent

Copyright © Sr. Dr. Vassa Larin
Vienna 2019

XENOPHON PRESS

Title:
Lent with Sister Vassa: Reflections for Every Day of Lent

ISBN: 9781948717397
Copyright © 2019 Sister Vassa Larin

All rights reserved. No part of this book may be reproduced, stored in a retrieval system, or transmitted in any form or by any means, electronic, mechanical, photocopying, recording, or otherwise, without the prior written permission of the author, except as provided by U.S.A. copyright law.

Published by Xenophon Press LLC
10237 Rogers Drive
Nassawadox Va 23413 USA
XenophonPress@gmail.com
1-757-442-1060

FOREWORD

This is a little book of daily reflections for Lent, the season of preparation for Easter or Pascha, according to the Byzantine liturgical calendar. I wrote it during the Lent of my very busy 2017, one day of Lent at a time, in the capital of Austria, Vienna, when I could not get to church-services often enough. Each reflection is on a topic either of one of the Scriptural readings of the day, or of the hymnography of the "Lenten Triodion," the Byzantine liturgical book that contains all the services concerning Lent.

I intend this book as a small offering to busy lay people, who may not have the time to "keep up" with the wealth of texts and services provided by the Byzantine tradition for Lent, but who, nonetheless, would like a daily, nurturing connection with the Church's Lenten "program" throughout their Lenten journey. May this book be helpful to you, my readers, as writing it was to me.

Chapter One: Pre-Lent

CHEESEFARE-SATURDAY
(of All Ascetical Fathers)

THE DOORS OF REPENTANCE

"Open to me the doors/gates (πύλας) of repentance, O Giver of Life: for early in the morning my spirit seeks Your holy temple, bearing a temple of the body all defiled. But in Your compassion cleanse it by Your loving-kindness and mercy." (Byzantine Hymn at Sunday Matins before and during Lent)

This pre-Lenten (and Lenten) hymn reminds me of "doors" that are presently closed. Otherwise I would not be asking for them to be opened. The fact is, I have closed the way leading to change, or "change of mind" ("metanoia" or repentance), having stagnated in certain, habitual patterns that "defile" (from "defouler," to trample down) or "trample down" my growth in God, the Giver of Life. And I need help, when it comes to making a change and opening those "doors" again, leading to change.

So this is an exciting time, this pre-Lenten season, which speaks primarily of change; a change I can enter into, when I pick up the simple tools laid out before me in the prayers, discipline, and atmosphere of Lent. It reminds me of the exciting time when John the Baptist first proclaimed a great change that was coming, as he "prepared the way of the Lord" and *"went into all the region around the Jordan, proclaiming a baptism of repentance for the forgiveness of sins..."* (Lk 3: 3) So let me join in and embrace this season of change; a change I can believe in.

FORGIVENESS SUNDAY
(Adam's Exile from Paradise)

GOD-FOCUSED FASTING

"And whenever you fast, do not look dismal, like the hypocrites, for they disfigure their faces so as to show people (τοῖς ἀνθρώποις) that they are fasting. Truly I tell you, they have received their reward. But when you fast, put oil on your head and wash your face, so that you do not appear as fasting to people (τοῖς ἀνθρώποις), but to your Father who is in secret; and your Father who sees in secret will reward you. Do not store up for yourselves treasures on

earth, where moth and rust consume and where thieves break in and steal; but store up for yourselves treasures in heaven, where neither moth nor rust consumes and where thieves do not break in and steal. For where your treasure is, there your heart will be also." (Mt 6: 16-21)

Fasting is good for me, no doubt about it. It is good for me both physically and spiritually. In fact today we fast more readily for physical reasons than for spiritual ones, I think, although both are interconnected and most effectively tackled together.

But in any event, it is bad for my heart to engage in fasting with "people" as my target audience. That is to say, it is disorienting for my heart, because people-pleasing makes me chase the changeable winds of human opinions, tastes, and expectations—including my own.

So let me dispense with "doing it for myself," as I am often advised, and with doing it for the "body image" considered most fashionable by people today. Let me rather have God as my target audience, as I care for my spiritual and physical "house," a treasure He entrusted to me. And let me prepare to fast according to my "vocation," which is comprised of all the various aspects of my life and character, with its strengths and weaknesses, known in their entirety only to God. I ask Him today to build with me this work-in-progress that is me, relying on His wisdom to develop and function properly. Let my heart be in Your hands, O Lord, like a treasure-in-progress in this fasting season. Amen!

Chapter Two: 1st Week of Lent

MONDAY, 1st WEEK (Clean Monday)

COME, LET US REASON TOGETHER

"Hear, O heaven, and hearken, O earth: for the Lord has spoken, saying, I have begotten and reared up children, but they have rebelled against me. The ox knows his owner, and the ass his master's crib: but Israel does not know me, and the people has not regarded me... Your fasting, and rest from work, your new moons also, and your feasts my soul hates: you have become loathsome to me; I will no more pardon your sins. When you stretch forth your hands, I will turn away my eyes from you: and though you make many supplications, I will not hearken to you; for your hands are full of blood. Wash you, be clean; remove your iniquities from your souls before my eyes; cease from your iniquities; learn to do well; diligently seek judgment, deliver him that is suffering wrong, plead for the orphan, and obtain justice for the widow. And come, let us reason together, saith the Lord: and though your sins be as purple, I will make them white as snow; and though they be as scarlet, I will make them white as wool..." (Is 1: 2-3, 14-18)

This is one of the readings for today, the first day of Lent. And what an unexpected reading it is. God tells us, among other things, "Your fasting...my soul hates." What kind of fasting does God's soul "hate"? The kind that is out of touch with Him and His purpose, which is to "remove iniquities" from our souls and "diligently" to "seek judgment" and "deliverance" for those "suffering wrong."

God seeks to make Himself "known" to us, so that we "come, and reason together" with His justice and mercy. He does this in part through external disciplines like fasts and feasts. Because these disciplines bring us together, out of self-isolation, and also slow us down, in our disparate and distracting pursuits. But they are not ends in themselves, and they lose their meaning outside of God. The "end" that God pursues, in slowing us down through fasting and feasting/resting periods, is our communion with Him, our harmony with His love and mercy.

So let me not lose sight of the forest, which is the "big" picture of God's all-encompassing justice and mercy, for the trees, which are the fasting-rules. We "ought" to follow the latter, as our Lord tells us, "without neglecting" the former (Mt 23: 23). As I begin the salvific discipline of Lent, let me "come and reason together" with God as He calls me to, in heartfelt prayer, and in humble reliance on His grace, so He can make my sins "white as snow" in and with Him. Happy beginning of Lent!

TUESDAY, 1st WEEK

GOD-GIVEN CHANGE

"And God said, 'Let there be lights in the firmament of the heavens to separate the day from the night; and let them be for signs and for seasons and for days and years, and let them be lights in the firmament of the heavens to give light upon the earth.' And it was so. And God made the two great lights, the greater light to rule the day, and the lesser light to rule the night; he made the stars also. And God set them in the firmament of the heavens to give light upon the earth, to rule over the day and over the night, and to separate the light from the darkness. And God saw that it was good. And there was evening and there was morning, a fourth day." (Gen 1: 14-19)

This is one of the readings for today, the second day of Lent. It redirects me, just like the rest of Lent, to the "basics" of my faith, which I tend to take for granted. Today I'm reminded of the basic, yet awe-inspiring fact that God created changeability and change. And He called it "good."

It is good for me that I experience God-given, physical transition and change all the time, which is beyond my control—from night to day, from midday to evening, from one month to the next, from winter to spring, from youth to adulthood, and so on. Because total monotony in our physical world would feel like a window-less prison cell.

But God also gives me a capacity to change in ways I can choose, according to my free will. I can step into His light and grow in Him, or I can self-isolate and stay in the shadows, doing whatever it is I want to do over there, on my own. But the great, liberating fact is, I don't have to do that. There is light, and today I can step right into it, in some heartfelt prayer and contemplation of His word. Because "the light shines in the darkness," also in my darkness today, "and the darkness has not overcome it." (Jn 1: 5)

WEDNESDAY, 1st WEEK

CRY OUT FOR DISCERNMENT

"For if you cry out for discernment, and lift up your voice for understanding; and if you seek it as silver, and search diligently for it as for treasures; then you will understand the fear of the Lord, and find the knowledge of God. For the Lord gives wisdom; and from his presence come knowledge and understanding, and he treasures up salvation for them that walk uprightly: he will protect their way;" (Prov 2: 3-7)

Discernment. Wisdom. Knowledge. Understanding. Are these the things I've been searching for "diligently, ...as for treasures"? At times, yes. But I need to be reminded, again and again, that these essential gifts, without which my life becomes utterly unmanageable, come from God. I must not only ask Him for them, but "cry out" for them when need be. Because I desperately need God to nudge me in the right direction, despite the weaknesses and distortions in my own vision of things.

Let me re-connect with, and stay close to, Him today, especially when I don't know what I'm doing, or what to do next. Because "from his presence come knowledge and wisdom." Help me, Lord, do the next right thing today, in Your presence and grace. Amen!

THURSDAY, 1ˢᵗ WEEK

IDLENESS & PROCRASTINATION

"O Lord and Master of my life, grant me not the spirit of idleness (ἀργίας, праздности), *despondency, lust of power, and idle talk* (ἀργο-λογίας, праздно-словия)." (Lenten Prayer of St. Ephrem, part 1)

Here the "spirit of idleness" or "ἀργία" (from "ἀ-εργία," literally "not working" or "not doing") means the bad kinds of "not doing." There are also good kinds of "not doing" (праздность) at certain, appropriate times (праздники), because we all need an occasional break in order to be restored. But here idleness means "not doing" what I am supposed to be doing, and when I am supposed to be doing it, according to my "vocation" or calling from God, specifically out of an avoidance and/or neglect of "responsibility" (i.e., my "response-ability" or my "ability to respond" to God's call). One such type of idleness is procrastination, e.g., when I have a pile of papers to grade, but opt to clean my desk instead.

What causes me to befriend the "spirit of idleness," including procrastination? Several things: 1. self-reliance, when I'm attempting to carry my responsibilities on my own shoulders, without God; 2. The resulting fear (of both failure and success) regarding the task at hand, which is too much for me alone; and 3. A loss of vision/sense of my "vocation," due to all-of-the-above.

So this morning let me replace fear with faith, and self-reliance with God-reliance, so I don't get stuck in self-centered, fear-inspired circles. Let me re-focus and listen for God's call to me, that I may respond in humble usefulness to myself and others. "Thy will be done" with me today, O Lord, according to Your purpose, whether I like it right now or not. Amen!

FRIDAY, 1st WEEK

GOD-FOCUSED HUNGER

"And Jesus, full of the Holy Spirit, returned from the Jordan, and was led by the Spirit for forty days in the wilderness, tempted by the devil. And he ate nothing in those days; and when they were ended, he was hungry. The devil said to him, 'If you are the Son of God, command this stone to become bread.' And Jesus answered him, 'It is written, 'Man shall not live by bread alone.'" (Lk 4: 1-4)

Jesus was, indeed, "hungry." He did, indeed, "need" something to eat. He also "could" provide bread for Himself in the wilderness, because this was within His power. Nonetheless, He rejects the devil's enticing suggestion, to turn a stone to bread. Why?

Because it's the devil's suggestion. And Christ is showing us that our God-given, physical needs, as well as our God-given powers, are not to be addressed outside God, as if they had a life of their own. We are called to train and exercise our needs and capacities in a God-focused way, as God wants, and not as the devil wants.

"Asceticism," from the Greek word "ἄσκησις," meaning "exercise, practice, training," in which we now engage during Lent, is a way to train and direct our human needs and divine capacities toward God's purpose and will, with His purpose and will in mind. By becoming a little more hungry and vulnerable, through fasting, we become more attentive to how and when we respond to our various hungers, both physical and spiritual.

Let me let myself be hungry today, in a God-focused manner. And when I eat, let me be attentive to "receiving" my food, rather than just taking it, according to a will that is not God's. *"Blessed are those who hunger and thirst for righteousness, for they will be satisfied."* (Mt 5: 6)

SATURDAY, 1ˢᵗ WEEK
(The Miracle of St. Theodore)

LORD OF THE SABBATH

"Again he entered the synagogue, and a man was there who had a withered hand. They watched him to see whether he would cure him on the sabbath, so that they might accuse

him. And he said to the man who had the withered hand, 'Come forward (εἰς τὸ μέσον, into the middle).' Then he said to them, 'Is it lawful to do good or to do harm on the sabbath, to save life or to kill?' But they were silent. He looked around at them with anger; he was grieved at their hardness of heart and said to the man, 'Stretch out your hand.' He stretched it out, and his hand was restored. The Pharisees went out and immediately conspired with the Herodians against him, how to destroy him.'" (Mk 3: 1-6)

So the Pharisees have murder in their hearts, seeking "to destroy" Jesus—and this unlawful desire they embrace on the sabbath. At the same time, they object to our Lord's insistence on "doing good" on the sabbath, like healing the man with the withered hand. This is why they are silent, when He asks them, *"Is it lawful to do good or to do harm on the sabbath, to save life or to kill?"* The Pharisees have so enslaved themselves (and others) to the external forms of the Law that they have no room in their hearts for its Spirit, Who is "Lord of the Sabbath" (cf. Mk 2: 28).

On this Saturday at the end of the first week of Lent, let me re-connect with the Lord of the Sabbath, opening my heart to His humble presence. However "good" or "bad" I am at following our fasting rules, let me not shut out His mercy, through formalistic demands of myself and/or others. I reach out to God, as one with a withered hand, unable "to do good" but by His grace.

1st SUNDAY OF LENT (of Orthodoxy)

I SAW YOU

"The next day Jesus decided to go to Galilee. And he found Philip and said to him, 'Follow me.' Now Philip was from Bethsaida, the city of Andrew and Peter. Philip found Nathanael, and said to him, 'We have found him of whom Moses in the law and also the prophets wrote, Jesus of Nazareth, the son of Joseph.' Nathanael said to him, 'Can anything good come out of Nazareth?' Philip said to him, 'Come and see.' Jesus saw Nathanael coming to him, and said of him, 'Behold, an Israelite indeed, in whom is no guile!' Nathanael said to him, 'How do you know me?' Jesus

answered him, 'Before Philip called you, when you were under the fig tree, I saw you.' Nathanael answered him, 'Rabbi, you are the Son of God! You are the King of Israel!'" (Jn 1: 43-49)

Nathaniel is weak in his reasoning, when he says, "Can anything good come out of Nazareth?"—as if nothing "good" can come out of a poor and insignificant town. He also seems to have a hard time accepting good news. But he is not insincere or hypocritical. And our Lord immediately praises this good in Nathaniel; the fact that in him there is "no guile," rather than point out his weaknesses. But Nathaniel, apparently, also has a hard time accepting praise, deflecting it with a question, "How do you know me?" So he's a hard nut to crack. Nathaniel does "come and see" the Lord, but "seeing" Christ was not enough for him.

It is only when Christ reveals to Nathaniel, "I saw you," that Nathaniel drops his defenses and professes Jesus as Teacher (rabbi), Son of God, and King of Israel. Because for many of us who are on the sidelines of faith, what wins us over to Christ is not "us" seeing "Him." Because He is revealing Himself all the time, but we may not have the eyes to see that. What wins us over, in an encounter with Christ, is receiving the assurance that "He" does, indeed, see "us," and know us, as we are, in our strengths and weaknesses. So let me "come and see" Christ, that I don't miss out on being seen, and known, by Him.

Chapter Three:
2nd Week of Lent

MONDAY, 2nd WEEK

A LIGHT BURDEN

"Come to me, all who labor and are heavy laden, and I will give you rest. Take my yoke upon you, and learn from me; for I am meek and humble in heart, and you will find rest for your souls. For my yoke is easy, and my burden is light." (Mt 11: 28-30)

As I enter the second week of Lent, I'm wondering whether Lent itself is part of the "burden" or "yoke" Christ is talking about. Is it?

Well, it can be, if it is "easy" and "light." Because that is how our Lord defines His "yoke" and "burden." He invites us to take these up in "meekness" and "humility in heart." So, if I take up Lent in meekness and humility, picking up its simple tools without needlessly debating how/whether they're right for me, I find that Lent brings me out of my own brand of "labor" and being "heavy laden," with its self-imposed "musts" and "needs." Lent gives me "rest" from my usual routine, offering me a routine not self-imposed, and filled with meaning and purpose. It is a meaning and purpose above and beyond my immediate stress, the meaning and purpose of which is not always clear.

This morning I once again embrace the meaning and purpose of Lent, which is a re-focusing on a God-centered life, a "change of mind" (metanoia) according to a humble self-acceptance, according to my God-given possibilities or "vocation." Lord, renew in me a right Spirit today, and help me learn from You, that I may find rest for my soul. Amen!

TUESDAY, 2nd WEEK

DRINKING FROM MY OWN WELL

"Drink water from your own cistern, flowing water from your own well. Should your springs be scattered abroad, streams of water in the streets? Let them be for yourself alone, and not for strangers with you. Let your fountain be blessed, and rejoice in the wife of your youth... Let her affection fill you at all times with

delight, be infatuated always with her love. Why should you be infatuated, my son, with a loose woman and embrace the bosom of an adventuress? For a man's ways are before the eyes of the Lord, and he (the Lord) watches all his paths." (Prov 5: 15-21)

Today, in our Internet Age, I can "drink water" from many available "wells," and also "scatter" my own all over the place. What does this mean? It means that I am easily distracted from my own vocation and tradition; from being of service and usefulness in the specific ways I am given, according to the upbringing, education, talents, people, situations, and other gifts I am given. I might forget even to speak with the person/s right in front of me, if my nose is in the little screen on my phone, constantly distracted "elsewhere."

Lent offers me a kind of "crash-course" in re-identifying with "the wife of my youth." (And yes, I realize the analogy is an awkward one, since I happen to be a woman. But please just work with me here.) The "wife of my youth" is my own Tradition, which has nurtured me, and cared for me, and continues to be there for me, reminding me of who I am, even at the times when I've looked "elsewhere." So today let me drink "from my own well," and re-focus on the abundant blessings I have in the here and now. Lord, help me be grateful and useful today, on the immediate paths You have set before me. Amen!

WEDNESDAY, 2nd WEEK

THE FAITH OF THE ATHEIST

"Now faith is the assurance of things hoped for, the conviction of things not seen. For by it the men of old received divine approval. By faith we understand that the world was created by the word of God, so that what is seen was made out of things which do not appear." (Heb 11: 1-3)

I'm thinking that the atheist view is also a faith, because it is a "conviction of things not seen." Because the atheist has "not seen" that God does not, indeed, exist. The atheist "faith" is not, however, an "assurance of things hoped for." It is a choice, rather, to close the door on all hope and on the ambivalences of mystery. Hence atheism tends to be sad, because it lacks hope, and it tends to be dull, because it lacks mystery. It is limited to man-made "understanding" like philosophy or mythology, while missing out on "divine approval," i.e., the voice of God to us.

Today I choose, once again, to embrace the ambivalence "of things hoped for." I embrace the adventure of mystery, both in my relationship with God and with others, all "made out of things that do not appear." May I be mindful today "of things not seen," by the grace of His word.

THURSDAY, 2nd WEEK

THINGS CHANGE

"And Adam knew his wife again, and she bore a son and called his name Seth, for she said, 'God has appointed for me another child instead of Abel, for Cain slew him.' To Seth also a son was born, and he called his name Enosh. At that time men began to call upon the name of the Lord." (Gen 4: 25-26)

It was only then, "at that time," after The Fall, that "men began to call upon the name of the Lord." Things changed.

I don't know the exact reason for the change at this specific moment—why it happened after Enosh was born to Seth, who was born to Eve after Cain killed Abel. But I do know from the Bible that "men began" a different kind of relationship with the Lord at that point, by calling upon His name. I'd like to reflect on the simple fact of that change.

Things changed back then, and they also continue to change today, when it comes to our relationship with God. Because Salvation History always tells us something about our own "history" with God. That's why Salvation History, recorded in the Bible, is relevant to me today, and why it is recorded in the first place, and continues to be passed on to all of us, throughout the generations, —because we "recognize" our own path in the paths made by the persons mentioned in the Bible. In the passage quoted above, I "recognize" that I also had times when I did not "call upon the name of the Lord," and when I "began," again, "to call upon" it. From reading the Bible-passage, I also receive the assurance and consolation that I am not the first to experience this change.

So today, if I find myself in the rut of "not" calling upon the name of the Lord, for whatever reason, let me be reminded that change is possible. I can "begin to call upon the name of the Lord," because He signals to me, through these messages in Scripture, that change is possible. Let me call upon His name today, however imperfectly, as many have before me, from the very beginning of our imperfect relationship with Him. *"O Lord, I have cried to you; hear me."*

FRIDAY, 2nd WEEK

IDLE WORDS

"O Lord and Master of my life, grant me not the spirit of idleness (ἀργίας, праздности), *despondency, lust of power, and idle talk / idle words* (ἀργολογίας, праздно-словия)." (Lenten Prayer of St. Ephrem, part 1)

It is important for us to talk and to share with one another our thoughts, sorrows, joys, and so on. No doubt about it. In fact I think we don't do enough of that today, when we are so often "alone together," even as a family, with each member staring into his or her computer/phone while sitting at the same table. Nonetheless, there is such a thing as "idle talk/words," so let me reflect on that a bit. What is it?

Just like "idleness" (ἀργία, from ἀ-ἐργία, or "not doing") means "not doing" what I am supposed to be doing, how, when and why I am supposed to be doing it, so does my "idle" use of words (ἀργο-λογία), whether spoken, written, or typed on my computer, mean my "not saying" what I am supposed to be saying, how, when and why I am supposed to be saying it, according to my vocation. So, "idle words" involve the inappropriate and untimely use of words, as well as their use with the wrong motivation. "Idle words" are always unconstructive, unproductive ones, which do more harm than good both to myself and others.

What are some of the "wrong" motivations for using words, and why are they harmful? I can, for example, "over-talk" about my certain aspirations or problems, out of self-assertion, self-justification, or self-pity. The harm in that is, I may be avoiding the silent contemplation of these issues; avoiding listening for the answers God may be sending me toward their further resolution, either through other people or otherwise. So I am blocking out the answers through my own words. I can similarly over-talk to God, motivated by the harmful assumption that my "many words" can or should manipulate His will. But my Lord warns me, *"And in praying do not heap up empty phrases as the Gentiles do; for they think that they will be heard for their many words..."* (Mt 6: 7)

So let me be reminded today of something I recently read (in the "Harvard Business Review," if you want to know). It's a bit of advice very useful in matters both practical and spiritual: "Silence is a greatly underestimated source of power... In silence, it can be easier to reach the truth." Let me stop my own words, when they cease to be of service, and become a bit more teachable, in silence and openness to God's voice in my life.

SATURDAY, 2nd WEEK
(of the reposed)

THE LIGHT OF LIFE

"Again Jesus spoke to them, saying, 'I am the light of the world; he who follows me will not walk in darkness, but will

have the light of life (τὸ φῶς τῆς ζωῆς).'" (Jn 8: 12)

What is "light"? In physical terms it is that which enables us to see. In theological terms it is God Himself, whose presence enables me to see things as they are, rather than how I wish or imagine them to be.

Let me not walk in darkness today, because I don't have to. "God is the Lord and has revealed Himself to us." (Ps 117: 27) Blessed is He Who comes, and blessed are we who receive Him, and choose to walk in His light and lightness.

2nd SUNDAY OF LENT
(of St. Gregory Palamas)

WE SHOULD HAVE SUCH A HIGH PRIEST

"For it was fitting that we should have such a High Priest (τοιοῦτος... ἀρχιερεύς), *holy, blameless, unstained, separated from sinners, exalted above the heavens. He has no need, like high priests* (ὥσπερ οἱ ἀρχιερεῖς), *to offer sacrifices daily, first for his own sins and then for those of the people; he did*

this once for all (ἐφάπαξ) when he offered up himself. Indeed, the law appoints men in their weakness as high priests, but the word of the oath, which came later than the law, appoints a Son who has been made perfect for ever." (Heb 7: 26-28)

We do, indeed, have many priests and "high" priests (e.g., bishops, archbishops, metropolitans, etc.). These are "men" appointed "in their weakness," and not "separated from sinners." But we only have One "such" High Priest, Who had no need to offer up "for" Himself, because He had no sin. He offered up, rather, Himself, and did so "once and for all" (ἐφάπαξ). And it is the human-divine person of Jesus Christ, with His unique, high-priestly ministry to all of us, that continues to be the Source of power and meaning for the "other" priests and high priests. Our "other" priests and high priests are no more, and indeed no less, than participants in a priesthood that is His alone.

I need this reminder every now and then, of Him Who is the basis of all our liturgical rites and rituals, lest I slip into some wrong approach to church-going.

One such "wrong" approach is a subtle consumerism, as if I am "fixing myself," as I see fit (whether I decide to approach confession, communion, and so on). Another false approach would be a focus/dependency on the personalities in church, as if the whole enterprise called "Church" was about human beings fixing or serving me. The power and "meaning of it all" remains, ever-perfectly, ever-stably, One "separated from sinners" and "exalted above the heavens." Today let me give up, once again, any attempts to "fix myself" or "be fixed" by human help alone. Even as I gratefully receive the ministry and help of priests in my church, I surrender to the will of One far greater than all of us, our Lord Jesus Christ, for it is "fitting," as St. Paul says, "that we should have such a High Priest."

Chapter 4: 3rd Week of Lent

MONDAY, 3rd WEEK

HUMILITY, AN ELUSIVE THING

"But grant unto me, Your servant, a spirit of chastity (σωφροσύνης, whole-mindedness, цело-мудрия), *humility* (ταπεινοφροσύνης, humble-mindedness, смиренно-мудрия), *patience and love."* (Lenten Prayer of St. Ephrem, part 2)

Humility is an elusive kind of thing, hard to define. It is also easy to mistake some "humility-counterfeit" for actual humility. For example, I might imagine I am being "humble," while actually escaping responsibility, according to my vocation, or donning a mask I have concocted, just not to be who I am called to be in my God-given place, time, and identity. As G. K. Chesterton famously noted, *"What we suffer from today is humility in the wrong place. Modesty has moved from the organ of ambition and settled upon the organ of conviction, where it was never meant to be. A man was meant to be doubtful about himself, but undoubting about the truth."*

The Lenten Prayer of St. Ephrem tells me three helpful things about humility: 1. It is good for me to ask for it, so I should desire it; 2. It is a "spirit," more specifically, it is an energy of the Holy Spirit, to which I open up, rather than something I should or can muster up from inside me; and 3. It is a "mindset" (ταπεινοφροσύνη, humble-mindedness, смиренно-мудрие) or "approach" to things, which involves a way of thinking. When I am "in" the grace of humble-mindedness, and the grace of humble-mindedness is "in" me, I find myself wisely able to "duck under the wave," in the Holy Spirit, when need be—of the dangerous wave or calamity that happens to come my way. So, humility is a "ducking under the wave," in the warm shelter and loving care of the Holy Spirit, rather than asserting my own, Spirit-less response to things. This does not always mean being silent, nor does it mean "being a doormat." It means asserting His energies, rather than my own. He becomes greater, and I become less. (cf. Jn 3: 30)

Today let me open up to God and His Spirit, staying close to Him, so that my response to situations, things, and people around me are softened and salted by humility, in His, and not my, wisdom. *"But grant unto me, Your servant, a Spirit of humble-mindedness."* Amen!

TUESDAY, 3rd WEEK

THE FORTY DAYS

"In the six hundredth year of Noah's life, in the second month, on the seventeenth day of the month, on that day all the fountains of the great deep burst forth, and the windows of the heavens were opened. And rain fell upon the earth forty days and forty nights." (Gen 7: 11-12)

Here's a strange thought. These "forty days and forty nights," mentioned in our Church's reading for today, during Lent, remind me of the 40 days of Lent. But is that really strange, to connect these two?

No, I don't think so. Because Scripture, along with other parts of Tradition, like Lent, is handed down to me, so I can make connections and "recognize" One-and-the-Same God working and speaking through it, yesterday and today. Certain symbols, like "forty days," repeat themselves here and there throughout Tradition, revealing a common language and common Source of that language, namely, God.

So, to get to my point, today I'm "connecting" the "forty days and forty nights" of rain falling upon the earth in The Great Flood with what is happening now, during Great Lent. In The Great Flood, God *"blotted out every living thing that was upon the face of the ground, man and animals and creeping things and birds of the air; they were blotted out from the earth. Only Noah was left, and those that were with him in the ark."* (Gen 7: 23) Now, during Lent, we are brought together in a special, extra-focused way in the ark that is the Church, experiencing a "flood" of God's grace in the intensified prayers, fasting, and other rituals of Lent. This "flood" is meant to "blot out" from my life all that has ceased to serve God's purpose. So I can re-focus, with others huddled together in our "ark," on His purpose, and then move on in a God-centered manner. Lord, give me shelter today in

Your ark, and blot out "every living thing," still living in me, which has ceased to serve You. Amen!

WEDNESDAY, 3rd WEEK

INTERNET PORN, THE "SECRET BREAD"

"A foolish and bold woman, who knows not modesty, comes to want a morsel. She sits at the doors of her house, on a seat openly in the streets, calling to passers by, and to those that are going right on their ways; saying, Whoever is most senseless of you, let him turn aside to me; and I exhort those that want prudence, saying, Take and enjoy secret bread, and the sweet water of theft. But one knows that mighty men die by her, and that one falls in with a snare of hell. But hasten away, delay not in the place, neither fix your eye upon her: for thus shall you go through strange water; but do abstain from strange water, and drink not of a strange fountain, that you may live long, and years of life may be added to you." (Prov 9: 13-18, Septuagint-translation)

So forgive the awkward topic. But this passage from Proverbs is part of our Church's reading for today, the third Wednesday of Lent, and it sheds some helpful light, I think, on the "secret bread" and secret torment of many today, also among Orthodox Christians—and that is, Internet pornography. Just recently I heard from an Orthodox priest that he hears quite a bit about this issue from Orthodox people at confession.

I think the above-quoted passage, while it was written over two millennia ago and wasn't talking about modern-day Internet-pornography, does expose its ugly "thinking" and spirit. Scripture is telling me here, this is "secret bread" and "strange water." It is both "bread" and "water," so it does satisfy a certain hunger, and quench a certain thirst. But it is "strange water," as well as "sweet water of theft," which is not healthy for me, or appropriate to my actual needs. It is an imposter, and a surrogate for fulfilling my God-given desires and drives. I am, indeed, given desires, also physical ones, from God, as is any human being, that I may grow and be useful to others and myself. So for a person of faith, desires and drives are to be discerned and channelled according to one's own, true vocation, and not according to the whims of "a foolish and bold woman," like Internet porn, who simply "comes to want a morsel" of us. I am not called to waste my will on imposters.

So let me not "delay in the place, neither fix my eye" on "the foolish and bold woman" that is Internet-pornography, that wants to "turn me aside to her" and waste my God-given desires and energies at her "strange fountain." And if she has lured me into sharing her dirty little secrets, let me expose this at confession, that I may "share" with her no more. O Lord, I turn my energies and will over to Your care today, that I may be useful to You, myself, and others, rather than waste my time. Amen!

THURSDAY, 3rd WEEK

OUR DAILY BREAD

"Give us this day our daily (τὸν ἐπιούσιον) *bread, and forgive us our trespasses, as we forgive those who trespass against us..."* (Mt 6: 11-12)

Yesterday I reflected on an unhealthy, deadly kind of "bread" that is Internet porn. Today I'd like to reflect on the vital, essential, "daily bread," suitable to our nature both now and in the life to come (according to the many explanations one finds in the Fathers, of the term "τὸν ἐπιούσιον"), which we are called to ask for and desire. One of the great things about Lent, I find, is that it teaches me to pay closer attention to my "food-choices," both physical and spiritual.

As far as physical "bread" goes, let me gratefully note that God provides it for me today. It includes the entirety of my physical needs, like food, shelter, clothing, face-to-face human fellowship, technology, etc. Gratitude steers me away from taking this "bread" for granted, or snatching up too much of it, or desiring "more," or desiring what others have, when I actually have enough. And forgiveness helps maintain my peace with my material situation, if anyone else "trespasses" against, or takes away, any of my "bread."

As far as healthy and vital spiritual "bread" goes, let me note that I easily lose sight of it altogether, overindulging in the wrong kind. I often allow myself to be fed "too much information" from news-sources or other media. (Do I really need to see more reports on a recent snow storm? On a misspelling in the President's tweets? On yet another so-and-so's opinion of the new healthcare bill?) I may be entirely exhausted and famished, without the essential "daily bread" I need, and not even notice it.

So today let me take pause, and take care of my health, both physical and spiritual. Let me re-connect with the Giver of Life and open up to His nurturing presence and grace, so abundantly on offer today, and every day. I take a bit of time for some deep, prayerful reading as well, that I may be nourished and strengthened through life-giving words, rather than exhausting and confusing ones. "Give us this day our daily bread, and forgive us our trespasses, as we forgive those who trespass against us." Amen!

FRIDAY, 3rd WEEK

THE SIXTH & NINTH HOUR

"And when the sixth hour had come, there was darkness over the whole land until the ninth hour. And at the ninth hour Jesus cried with a loud voice, 'E'lo-i, E'lo-i, la'ma sabach-tha'ni?' which means, 'My God, my God, why have you forsaken me?' And some of the bystanders hearing it said, 'Behold, he is calling Elijah.' And one ran and, filling a sponge full of vinegar, put it on a reed and gave it to him to drink, saying, 'Wait, let us see whether Elijah will come to take him down.' And Jesus uttered a loud cry, and breathed his last. And the curtain of the temple was torn in two, from top to bottom. And when the centurion, who stood facing him, saw that he thus breathed his last, he said, 'Truly this man was the Son of God!'" (Mk 15: 33-39)

On this third Friday of Lent, I'd like to remember that Friday over two millennia ago, when things so radically changed between us and God. The "curtain of the temple," which separated the Holy of Holies, God's earthly dwelling-place, from the rest of the temple where human beings dwelt, was "torn in two." The separation between us and God was being overcome in Christ's death. He had taken on our "sin," which separated us from God, and its consequence, death, darkness, and even despair, in order to "trample" all that and bring us out of it, in Him.

How is it that He brings "us" out of it, and not only Himself? Because He shares our humanity, our human nature, having become man. We share an underlying oneness, a connection, from human being to human being, both physical and spiritual, although it is easy to lose sight of this fact amidst our divisions. Our spiritual connection is our one-and-only Creator, God's Spirit Who breathed life into us. Our physical connection, already obvious in the scientific fact that our genetic make-up is 99.9 percent identical, is made profoundly more intimate in the Body of Christ, of which He invites us to partake in Holy Communion.

Today in my "sixth hour" (i.e., midday) and in my "ninth hour" (3 o'clock in the afternoon) let me take pause and remember the "darkness over the whole land," the "loud voice" of the God Man, crying out in our despair, and the "tearing in two" of that curtain of separation, through my Lord's "last" breath. *"In the ninth hour, You tasted death in the flesh for our sake, O Christ God. Put also to death our carnal mind* (thinking according to the flesh, τῆς σαρκὸς ἡμῶν τὸ φρόνημα, плоти нашея мудрование), *and save us!"* (Byzantine Troparion of the Ninth Hour)

SATURDAY, 3rd WEEK
(of the reposed)

THE ROSE AND CAME HOME

"And as he passed on, he saw Levi the son of Alphaeus sitting at the tax office, and he said to him, 'Follow me.' And he rose and followed him. And as he sat at table in his house, many tax collectors and sinners were sitting with Jesus and his disciples; for there were many who followed him. And the scribes and the Pharisees, when they saw that he was eating with sinners and tax collectors, said to his disciples, 'Why does he eat with tax collectors and sinners?' And when Jesus heard it, he said to them, 'Those who are well (οἱ ἰσχύοντες) *have no need of a physician, but those who are sick* (οἱ κακῶς ἔχοντες); *I*

came not to call the righteous, but sinners to repentance (εἰς μετάνοιαν)." (Mk 2: 14-17)

So Levi, one of the "sinners" in this picture, was called to "repentance" ("metanoia," a change of mind, change of focus). What did "repentance" look like, in his case? First, Levi "rose" from where he was sitting. Then he "followed" Christ, Who led him back into his own home. And there Levi "ate" with his fellow-tax-collectors and sinners, together with the Lord.

Lord, I am, once again, "in need of a physician" today, where I am sitting, outside my true "home." So once again I hear Your call: I "rise" and let You lead me back where I belong, "at table" and in fellowship with You and my fellow-sinners.

3rd SUNDAY OF LENT
(Veneration of the Cross)

BEING ALONE vs. BEARING MUCH FRUIT

"And he called to him the multitude with his disciples, and said to them, 'If any man wants to come after me, let

him deny himself and take up his cross and follow me. For whoever would save his life/soul (τὴν ψυχὴν αὐτοῦ) *will lose it; and whoever loses his life/soul for my sake and the gospel's will save it. For what does it profit a man, to gain the whole world and forfeit his life/soul? For what can a man give in return for his life/soul?'"* (Mk 8: 34-37)

This doesn't make much sense, this talk about "losing" my "life/soul" in order to "save" it—does it? Well, it does, if I remember that our Lord distinguishes between two kinds of "life/soul": 1. the kind we all have whether we want it or not, just by being born of our physical parents; and 2. The kind we can embrace "if we want to come after Him," denying a self-isolated existence outside of Him, and joining Him on the life-giving journey of the Cross. *"Truly, truly, I say to you," "unless a grain of wheat falls into the earth and dies, it remains alone; but if it dies, it bears much fruit. He who loves his life/soul loses it, and he who hates his life/soul in this world will keep it for eternal life."* (Jn 12: 24-25)

So let me join Him today, once again, on the cross-carrying adventure that brings me Life with a capitol "L." Let me "lose" the self-centeredness and self-seeking that aims, quite pointlessly, "to gain the whole world." I rather take up my cross today, walking through my immediate responsibilities, as He calls me to, in my here and now. God sends me this cross, which "saves" or "heals" my "life/soul," as He sees fit. "Thy will be done" with me today, O Lord, that I not "remain alone," but "bear much fruit."

Chapter Five: 4th Week of Lent

MONDAY, 4th WEEK

EXTERNAL & INTERNAL BEAUTY

"As a ring in the snout of a pig, so is beauty in an ill-minded woman." (Prov 11: 22, Septuagint-translation)

Wow, that's harsh. But wait a minute, and let's think about what this passage says about physical beauty in human beings. Because it is talking about physical beauty in a person—not only a woman—whose internal disposition ("mind") is "ill." If you want to argue with that interpretation, and insist that this passage refers only to women, then go ahead and argue that the very first words of the Psalter, *"Blessed is the man..."* (Ps 1: 1), refer only to "men." If you will not argue that, then let's dispense with gender-specifics and talk about physical beauty in people in general.

Physical "beauty" in human beings attracts us to them, at a first glance, if we are not blind. But if we proceed to discover they are "ill-minded" in some way, then the contrast between their external appearance and their inner character ("mind") is particularly off-putting. Like "a ring in the snout of a pig." It isn't very "fair" to beautiful people, I suppose, but that is the way it is.

In our time of relative affluence, with our access to modern-day medicine, beauty-products, fitness-clubs, and healthy food, I think many of us have the opportunity to be more or less "beautiful" physically. But let me be reminded today—if I do enjoy this gift of physical beauty and care for it—of an ancient, simple wisdom from Holy Scripture. And that is, that physical beauty in a human being is not meant to be out of harmony with his/her spiritual beauty. Let me care for my inner "mind," that it not be "ill" but aligned with God, the Source of Beauty, in heartfelt prayer, contemplation of His word, and self-examination. Let me take care of all that, before I head for the gym, or do my hair, or take care of my outer appearance in some other way. Lord, help me keep things in perspective, that I may be healthy and beautiful in Your eyes. Amen!

TUESDAY, 4th WEEK

GOD'S MANY SIGNS

"And the Lord God said to Noah, This is the sign of the covenant which I set between me and you, and between every living creature which is with you for perpetual generations. I set my rainbow in the cloud, and it shall be for a sign of covenant between me and the earth. And it shall be when I gather clouds upon the earth, that my rainbow shall be seen in the cloud. And I will remember my covenant, which is between me and you, and between every living soul in all flesh, and there shall no longer be water for a flood, so as to blot out all flesh." (Gen 9: 12-15)

So, a "rainbow in a cloud" is a special "sign of covenant," of a certain kind of agreement, understanding, or, simply put, "connection" that God has with us. Really there are countless "signs" in God's created world, which point us to Him as our common Creator, if we have the eyes to see. But we don't always have those eyes, as Simon and Garfunkel note in their brilliant song, *"My Little Town"*: *"And after it rains, there's a rainbow, / And all of the colors are black, / It's not that the colors aren't there, / It's just imagination they lack, / Everything's the same back / In my little town."*

Today I'm reminded that God has His "signs" all over the place, as the Holy Spirit continues to "rain" and pour out His mercy most abundantly on "my little town." Everything is never "the same," from day to day, in the abundance of "colors" God shows me in the people, places and things He brings my way. Let me be both grateful and teachable today, that I can learn more about His presence and grace in our midst.

WEDNESDAY, 4th WEEK

COVERING YOUR FATHER'S NAKEDNESS

"Now the sons of Noah which came out of the ark, were Sem, Ham, Japheth. And Ham was father of Canaan. These three are the sons of Noah, of these were men scattered over all the earth. And Noah began to be a husbandman, and he planted a vineyard. And he drank of the wine, and was drunk, and was naked in his house. And Ham the father of

Canaan saw the nakedness of his father, and he went out and told his two brothers outside. And Sem and Japheth having taken a garment, put it on both their backs and went backwards, and covered the nakedness of their father; and their face was backward, and they saw not the nakedness of their father. And Noah recovered from the wine, and knew all that his younger son had done to him. And he said, Cursed be the servant Canaan, a slave shall he be to his brethren." (Gen 9: 18-25)

This important passage from Genesis, which talks about Ham's sin of "not covering" his father's nakedness, but rather "telling his brothers outside," is read only once a year in the Byzantine liturgical calendar, on this Wednesday of the fourth week of Lent. So let me reflect on it.

In Russian, the word that means "disrespect for one's elders" is "ham-stvo" ("hamishness"); it is named after Ham. When we use this word in Russian, we usually mean explicit rudeness, like talking back to one's parents or some other superior/authority. But what Ham did is more subtle. Having "seen" the nakedness of his father, he went "outside" and talked about it to his peers, his two brothers. Ham's sin is not the "seeing" part, because he did not expect to find his father naked when he walked into Noah's house. His sin is that he lacked the compassion to cover the unexpected shame of Noah, his father, who was the first to experience the effects of wine, and quite innocently "overdid it" when he tried it. He was not some alcoholic father who regularly abused the substance, beat up on his children, or anything like that. Noah was rather a man who had just saved his entire family in an ark that he built, according to the will of God, Who deemed Noah—and Noah alone—worthy to do so. Ham could have at least covered up "the nakedness" of this great man in his predicament. But that is not what Ham did. So Ham's own son is "cursed," because our children will tend to repeat our own lack of compassion and sensitivity to our parents.

I am sometimes given to "see" some shortcoming of my parents, superiors and elders. Let me take pause, however, before I talk about them "outside." The least I can do, I think, for the great people who have nurtured me and cared for me in their "ark," is gently to cover up their "nakedness," when need be, as I would want mine to be covered up by those dependent on me, when it is revealed. O Lord, forgive us, as we forgive. Amen!

THURSDAY, 4ᵗʰ WEEK

PLACING HOPE IN FALSEHOOD

"Therefore hear the word of the Lord, afflicted people, and rulers of the people that are in Jerusalem. Because you have said, We have made a covenant with Hades, and agreements with death; if the rushing storm should pass, it shall not come upon us: we have made falsehood our hope, and by falsehood shall we be protected: Therefore thus says the Lord, even the Lord, Behold, I lay for the foundations of Sion a costly stone, a choice, a corner-stone, a precious stone, for its foundations; and he that believes on him shall by no means be ashamed. And I will cause judgment to be for hope, and my compassion shall be for just measures, and you that trust vainly in falsehood shall fall: for the storm shall by no means pass by you, except it also take away your covenant of death, and your trust in Hades shall by no means stand: if the rushing storm should come upon you, you shall be beaten down by it." (Is 28: 14-18, Septuagint-transaltion)

To place trust or hope "in falsehood" is a bad policy, both for "rulers of people" in their governing, and for each of us in our personal lives. And by "falsehood" I mean various kinds of wishful thinking, about myself or others. This includes pretending to be who I am not, because of people-pleasing and fear, and imagining or expecting from others to be who/what they are not, according to my self-will alone. A "rushing storm," if it happens to come upon us, will bring down this house of cards.

I cannot "see" the truth about anything, actually, outside God and His light, because in my own, limited head I tend to "miss the mark." As Christ reminds the Pharisees, *"If you were blind, you would have no sin; but now that you say, 'We see,' your sin remains."* (Jn 9: 41) So today I let Christ, the Word of God, be the "precious corner-stone" in the foundations of my "house," that I may be protected in His humbling light, and in my blindness. *"The stone which the builders rejected has become the head corner-stone. This is the Lord's doing, and it is marvelous in our eyes."* (Ps 117/118: 22-23)

FRIDAY, 4th WEEK

SHARERS IN EVERLASTING LIFE

"Now the powers of heaven minister invisibly with us. For, behold, the King of Glory enters. Behold the mystical sacrifice, fully accomplished, is ushered in. Let us draw near in faith and love, that we may become sharers/partakers (μέτοχοι, причастники) *in everlasting life. Alleluia, alleluia, alleluia."* (Liturgy of the Presanctified Gifts, Great Entrance hymn)

This is the hymn we sing at the Lenten Liturgy of the Presanctified Gifts, when the "mystical sacrifice" of the Body and Blood of Christ, the already-consecrated Gifts (consecrated at the Divine Liturgy of the previous Sunday), are transferred in a solemn procession from the Prothesis-table to the Holy Table in the altar. Here the unity of "us" with "the powers of heaven," of the earthly and the heavenly, the temporal and everlasting, is stressed, just as it is in the Byzantine Divine Liturgy. Why? Because the Body of Christ brings all of creation together, the visible and invisible.

So let me "draw near," as I am invited to do, that I may be a "sharer" or "partaker" not just of "life and life only" (in the words of Bob Dylan), but of "everlasting life," which extends above and beyond my smallness and brokenness. I am invited to share in the Body of Christ—consecrated, broken, and given for me. So let me share in His brokenness, that I may be restored to wholeness, visible and invisible. Amen!

SATURDAY, 4ᵗʰ WEEK (of the reposed)

UNREFLECTING FAITH

"In the sixth month the angel Gabriel was sent from God to a city of Galilee named Nazareth, to a virgin betrothed to a man whose name was Joseph, of the house of David; and the virgin's name was Mary. And he came to her and said, 'Hail, O full of grace (κεχαριτωμένη), *the Lord is with you! Blessed are you among women!' But she was greatly troubled at the saying, and considered in her mind what sort of greeting this might be."* (Lk 1: 26-29)

Mary was not an un-reflecting kind of person. She was "greatly troubled" by, and "considered in her mind" what in the world an angel—yes, an angel, no less—was talking about. She needed to know more, because the "greeting" made no sense in the context of Mary's life-experience thus far.

I'm thinking about this today, because I just read something that disturbed me in the works of the famous psychologist, Karl Jung, about us church-people often having "un-reflecting faith." This is what Jung observes: *"The Churches stand for traditional and collective convictions which in the case of many of their adherents are no longer based on their own inner experience but on un-reflecting faith, which is notoriously apt to disappear as soon as one begins thinking about it."* I was disturbed by Jung's observation, because I think he is right. I mean, it seems to me he is right as far as we, the people of my Church today, are concerned.

I'm consoled, however, by the example of the Blessed Among Women, in those early times of our "traditional and collective convictions," when the Holy Virgin was being introduced to them. She does "consider in her mind," and have questions, but also has an open heart to the replies of God's messenger, Gabriel.

So let me not hesitate today, to "consider in my mind" what it is God is telling me through His many messengers, including the people and situations He sends my way. This does not have to be a complicated process, in connection with His grace, when I connect with Him in heartfelt prayer. It is simple, even though it is not easy. Let me have an open heart to God's replies, in my God-given conscience.

4th SUNDAY OF LENT (of St. John Climacus)

THE DEAF AND DUMB SPIRIT

"And when Jesus saw that a crowd came running together, he rebuked the unclean spirit, saying to it, 'You dumb and deaf spirit, I command you, come out of him, and never enter him again.' And after crying out and convulsing him terribly, it came out, and the boy was like a corpse; so that most of them said, 'He is dead.' But Jesus took him by the hand and lifted him up, and he arose. And when he had entered the house, his disciples asked him privately, 'Why

could we not cast it out?' And he said to them, 'This kind cannot be driven out by anything but prayer and fasting.'" (Mk 9: 25-29)

A "deaf and dumb spirit" afflicts me when I am unable to say what I need to say, for example, at confession, and hear what I need to hear, in open-hearted teachability. This kind of spirit traps me in circles of self-isolation and self-justification, doing the same self-destructive thing over and over again. So it was for the boy healed by Jesus, as the boy's father testifies: The spirit, says the father, *"has often cast him into the fire and into the water, to destroy him..."* (Mk 9: 22)

This Lent, let me come before my Lord and have this spirit cast out "by prayer and fasting." And I don't mean my own prayer and fasting, because I can't cast out my own demons, even if I were the world-champion of prayer and fasting. I mean, the prayer and fasting of the Church in this wonderful season, which offers me healing and liberation from my demons, if only I am willing to come and be healed. So let me come and be healed, in heartfelt confession and teachability. Lord, lift me up, that I may rise, by the prayers of Your holy Church. Amen!

Chapter 6: 5th Week of Lent

MONDAY, 5th WEEK

WHY "FEAR" GOD?

"In the fear of the Lord is strong confidence: and he leaves his children a support. The commandment of the Lord is a fountain of life; and it causes men to turn aside from the snare of death." (Prov 14: 26-27, Septuagint-translation)

"Fear" is a life-giving, God-given gift, essential for survival. It is an evolved capacity in the human being, so science tells us. But like other God-given gifts and drives, which I inherently have as a human being, fear becomes harmful to me when it is divorced from God; when it is not "of God" and takes on a life of its own. Inherent, human fear in a life not God-focused is crippling, existential anxiety in the face of the many uncertainties and ambivalences that are part-and-parcel of any human life.

"In the fear of the Lord," I am reminded as I begin the fifth week of Lent, "is strong confidence." I "fear" losing my connection with Him and focus on

Him, the Source of love, wisdom, and forgiveness of my sins, and this "fear of the Lord" liberates me from merely-human fears, of financial insecurity, of human opinion, of loneliness, and so on. "I walk the line" He sets out before me today, in the situations, work, and relationships I am given in my particular vocation, or "commandment of the Lord." So let me do the next right thing today, according to His call—that is, according to my immediate responsibilities. Let my vocation be what it is meant to be today, "a fountain of life," which causes me "to turn aside from the snare of death."

TUESDAY, 5th WEEK

DOES THE THEOTOKOS "SAVE" US?

"Most Holy Theotokos, save us!" (Byzantine prayer)

What, exactly, are we asking for in this prayer? Are we calling for another human being, Mary, to "save" us, as only our One Saviour and Lord Jesus Christ can?

No. We are calling for the "Birth-Giver of God" in the flesh, the "Theo-tokos," in Her unique ministry of bringing Him into the world, to bring us His salvation. He willed it to "save" the world in His incarnation, coming to us through Her over 2,000 years ago. And we believe in Him as in One Who continues to come to us, to "come again" and again (καὶ πάλιν ἐρχόμενον, и паки грядущаго) as the incarnate Lord.

Thus when we say, "Most Holy Theotokos, save us!"—and not "Mary, save us!"—we are calling also upon His name, the name of "God" incarnate, Who has brought us His salvation not without Her. We thus embrace that great mystery, of the Incarnation, when we say this today, because that mystery continues to work its salvific consequences in His One Body that is the Church. "Most Holy Theotokos, save us!" I say today, embracing His coming as He does, not only spiritually, but also physically, into holy communion with us.

WEDNESDAY, 5th WEEK

THE GREAT CANON OF ST. ANDREW

"Two men went up into the temple to pray, one a Pharisee and the other a tax collector. The Pharisee stood and prayed thus with himself, 'God, I thank you that I am not like other men, extortioners, unjust, adulterers, or even like this tax collector. I fast twice a week, I give tithes of all that I get.' But the tax collector, standing far off, would not even lift up his eyes to heaven, but beat his breast, saying, 'God, be merciful to me a sinner!'" (Lk 18: 10-13)

Tonight in our churches we will be hearing the very long, "Great" Canon of St. Andrew of Crete. It contains many, many words: beautiful lamentations, biblical references, theological insights, and so on. It can be hard for us, with our present-day short attention-spans, to "follow" every word of this Canon. But the refrain to the Canon, repeated throughout the service, is easy to follow: *"Have mercy on me, O God, have mercy on me."* It reminds me of the simple prayer of the tax-collector in the parable quoted above, which we read in our churches at the very beginning of the Lenten season.

Let me keep things simple today, and open my heart to God's mercy. I give up and surrender to Him, approaching Him with nothing, in my lack of understanding and everything else. Because God has, where I lack. *"Have mercy on me, O God, have mercy on me."*

THURSDAY, 5th WEEK

WALKING ON PATHS UNKNOWN

"The Lord God of hosts shall go forth, and crush the war: he shall stir up jealousy, and shall shout mightily against his enemies... '...I will bring the blind by a way that they knew not, and I will cause them to walk paths which they have not known: I will turn darkness into light for them, and crooked things into straight. These things I will do, and will not forsake them. But they are turned back: be you utterly ashamed that trust in graven images, who say to the molten images, You are our gods.'" (Is 42: 13, 16-17, Septuagint-translation)

I am often shocked, really, by the very "human" expressions of God's divine zeal for saving us, His people. "I will do these things," He promises, "and will not forsake" you: "I will turn darkness into light" for you, He says, "and crooked things into straight." He will also "bring the blind," like me, "by a way that they knew not," and "will cause them to walk paths which they have not known."

But I should not be shocked, really, by God's willingness to do all this for me. Because He has done it already, time and again, in my life. So today, if I face the "darkness" of some uncertainties in life, or "paths which I have not known," or "crooked things,"— whether at work, in personal relationships, or elsewhere—let me not be "turned back" to God's loving, zealous willingness to lead me through it, as He always has. Thy will be done with me today, O Lord, as it was yesterday. Amen!

FRIDAY, 5th WEEK

REMEMBERING DEATH

"My soul, my soul, arise! Why are you sleeping? The end is drawing near, and you will be confounded. Awake, then,

and be watchful, that Christ our God may spare you, Who is everywhere present and fills all things." (Kontakion-hymn, Great Canon of St. Andrew)

Whether we like it or not, our mortality, or the fact that we will all, indeed, die a physical death, is something with which we are confronted more and more as we age. This fact really begins to "hit home" for many of us when we lose a parent, or notice our parents aging. Psychologists observe that such reminders of our own mortality often cause depression, existential angst, and various unhealthy behaviors in middle-aged people in our time.

But there is nothing morbid or dark in "remembering death," as we are taught to do regularly in our beautiful Tradition. Here's the paradoxical thing about actively remembering death: It makes me more "watchful" and "awake" to life. I learn to pay attention more, to the presence of God in my here and now, in the people, places, and situations I am given today from Him, "Who is everywhere present and fills all things." I learn not to miss out on what I am called to do in the today, in usefulness to myself and others, rather than let life pass by and just "happen," as John Lennon said, "when you're not paying attention."

Let me "awake, then, and be watchful," on this sunny Friday. *"I shall not die, but live, and I shall tell of the works of the Lord."* (Ps 117/118: 17)

SATURDAY, 5th WEEK

CAN'T START A FIRE WITHOUT A SPARK

"...And Mary said to the angel, 'How shall this be, since I have no husband?' And the angel said to her, 'The Holy Spirit will come upon you, and the power of the Most High will overshadow you; therefore the child to be born will be called holy, the Son of God. And behold, your kinswoman Elizabeth in her old age has also conceived a son; and this is the sixth month with her who was called barren. For with God nothing will be impossible.' And Mary said, 'Behold, I am the handmaid of the Lord; let it be to me according to your word.' And the angel departed from her.'" (Lk 1: 34-37)

The unsung hero of this story, I think, is the Holy Spirit. It is He Who enables a teen-aged virgin from Nazareth, despite Mary's questions and confusion in the face of the strange news of the archangel, to conceive and give birth to the eternal Word of God in this world.

Now, please forgive me for some unconventional thoughts on this central moment in Salvation History. But it reminds me in general of our human, creative process. It is impossible to conceive, and give birth to, anything good in this world, I think, without that "spark" of the Holy Spirit. As Bruce Springsteen notes in his profound song about his own writing-process (Dancing in the Dark): "I ain't nothing but tired," he says, "Man I'm just tired and bored with myself / ...I could use just a little help / You can't start a fire without a spark..."

As we praise and magnify the Most-Holy Theotokos today, on this wonderful Saturday of the Akathist, let me embrace the Holy Virgin's openness to, and faith in, the Holy Spirit, with Whom "nothing will be impossible." I re-connect with Him today, in heartfelt prayer, as I approach my work, rather than isolate myself from God's creative energies in self-reliance, being "bored with myself." *"Behold, I am the handmaiden of the Lord; let it be to me according to your word."* Amen!

5th SUNDAY OF LENT
(of St. Mary of Egypt)

FORGIVEN FOR LOVE

"...Then turning toward the woman he (Jesus) said to Simon (the Pharisee), 'Do you see this woman? I entered your house, you gave me no water for my feet, but she has wet my feet with her tears and wiped them with her hair. You gave me no kiss, but from the time I came in she has not ceased to kiss my feet. You did not anoint my head with oil, but she has anointed my feet with ointment. Therefore I tell you, her sins, which are many, are forgiven, for she loved much; but he who is forgiven little, loves little.'" (Lk 7: 44-47)

This sinful woman "loved much," says the Lord. But who is it that this woman "loved much"? It is interesting to me that our Lord does not specify. It is clear from her actions that she loved our Lord "much." But He says about her, generally, that she "loved much." Because, I suspect, she generally "loved much," and gave of herself wholeheartedly, often irrationally, to others. She did this in love—with all that love entails, like forgiving other sinners, perhaps her many lovers, who may have "trespassed against" her all the time, in her sinful life. This "loving much," as awkward as it was in the life of this woman, does not go unnoticed by the One Who knows our hearts. He gives her a break and says to her, *"Your sins are forgiven,"* and *"Your faith has saved you; go in peace."* (Lk 7: 48, 50)

This passage is a great consolation for those of us who have "loved much," even "too" much, and perhaps irrationally, making spectacles of ourselves, in love, as does this woman in the house of Simon the Pharisee. We can and do turn to the Lord of our hearts, with our tears, and are forgiven, even before we can forgive ourselves. *"O Lord, I have cried unto You. Hear me!"* (Ps 140/141: 1)

Chapter Seven: 6th Week of Lent

MONDAY, 6th WEEK

CALLED TO BE OURSELVES

"For many are called (κλητοὶ), but few are chosen." (Mt 22: 14)

A "calling" or "vocation" is common to all members of the "church" or "ekklesia" (from the Greek verb "ekkaleo," which means "to call out"). We are all "called" "according to his purpose" (Rom 8: 28) for each of us, according to our specific, God-given gifts and character. But it is not easy to discern God's voice in our lives (our specific "calling"), because we are burdened with other voices. They pull us away from being ourselves, the "selves" God wants us to be, and into a mainstream of popular masks behind which most of us feel safe.

A "vocation," as Karl Jung defines it, is "an irrational factor that destines a man to emancipate himself from the herd and from its well-worn paths." That is to say, it is liberating. But Jung also notes that "vocation" is "at once a charisma and a curse, because its first fruit is the conscious and unavoidable segregation of the single individual from the undifferentiated and unconscious herd. That means isolation..."

Let me ask God for courage today, to be myself, as He made me and sees me, that I may be liberated from wearing masks or trying to be someone else. Let me choose His voice today, that I may be "chosen" and liberated by Him, to be myself.

TUESDAY, 6th WEEK

KILL YOUR DARLINGS

"Wretched daughter of Babylon! ... Blessed shall he be who shall seize and dash your infants against the rock." (Ps 136/137: 8a, 9, Septuagint-translation)

In his little book "On Writing," the great novelist Stephen King uses a similar image to advise the inexperienced writer about the painful editing process: "Kill your darlings," he says. He means that the writer should not hesitate to cross out (or delete) all unnecessary details, no matter how much he or she loves them.

The Psalm is also talking about "infants" that I tend to love, within myself. They are sinful thoughts, at first small and weak, of various types of wishful thinking, lustful thinking, fearful thinking, resentful thinking, and so on. These "infants" need to be "dashed" against the "rock,"—my Rock and my Hope, Jesus Christ. May I get rid of any creepy "infants" today and let Him take care of them, before they grow and take over my house. "Lord Jesus Christ, Son of God," be my Rock today. Amen.

WEDNESDAY, 6th WEEK

THE HOPE OF THE RESURRECTION

"Almighty Lord, You have created all things in wisdom. In Your inexpressible providence and great goodness You have brought us to these saving days, for the cleansing of our souls and bodies, for control of our passions, in the hope of the Resurrection. After the forty days You delivered into the hands of Your servant Moses the tablets of the law in characters divinely traced. Enable us also, O benevolent One, to fight the good fight, to complete the

course of the fast, to keep the faith inviolate, to crush underfoot the heads of unseen tempters, to emerge victors over sin and to come, without reproach, to the worship of Your Holy Resurrection. For blessed and glorified is Your most honorable and majestic name..." (Lenten Liturgy of Presanctified Gifts, Opisthambonos-Prayer)

The "forty days" of Lent will end this Friday, because the upcoming days of Holy/Great Week (Страстная неделя) do not "count" as part of the forty, standing in a class of their own. Just a fun fact, in case you didn't know.

As the end of the forty days draws near, I'm particularly encouraged by one phrase in the above-quoted prayer: "the hope of the Resurrection." This hope is what keeps us going—not only through Lent, but also through our cross-carrying journeys in general. It is not a hope that remains entirely unfulfilled in our earthly lives. As St. Gregory Palamas teaches us, we experience "a foretaste of the bodily resurrection" as we participate in the divine energies of God's grace in the here and now.

His grace is abundantly on offer today, not blocked off from me. So let me open up to Him in simple, heartfelt prayer, as Pascha draws near. O Lord, enable us also *"to come, without reproach, to the worship of Your Holy Resurrection."* Amen!

THURSDAY, 6ᵗʰ WEEK

CHRIST'S FINAL WORD

"Now a certain man was ill, Lazarus of Bethany, the village of Mary and her sister Martha… So the sisters (of Lazarus) sent to him, saying, 'Lord, he whom you love is ill.' But when Jesus heard it he said, 'This illness is not unto death; it is for the glory of God, so that the Son of God may be glorified by means of it.' Now Jesus loved Martha and her sister and Lazarus. So when he heard that he was ill, he stayed two days longer in the place where he was." (Jn 11: 1, 3-5)

Jesus "loved" Lazarus and his two sisters, these simple people, not extolled for any special virtue in the Gospels. Just as He loves all of us, for whom He died on the Cross "while we were still sinners" (Rom 5: 8). But when our Lord heard about Lazarus's deadly illness, which was so dire that

Martha and Mary sent Him word of it, He "stayed two days longer in the place" where He was, not rushing over to Bethany to heal His good friend. The Son of God knew that Lazarus would die from this illness, but that his illness would, nonetheless, not be "unto death." Because death would not have "the final word" concerning Lazarus. The "final word" was that of the life-giving Word of God, Jesus Christ, Who was to raise His beloved friend from the dead several days later, saying, "Lazarus, come out!"

Nor does death have "the final word" concerning all of us, in the love of Christ. Because Christ has embraced us all, with His hands outstretched in His own "illness" on the Cross. But Christ's suffering was "not unto death," just as Lazarus's wasn't, even though both Christ and Lazarus truly died a physical death. And so are our illnesses and suffering "not unto death," when we embrace His word, in love. Even "while we are still sinners," in our imperfections.

So let me look death in the face today, and recognize that it no longer has "the final word" in my life. It has been vanquished by the love and friendship of my Lord Jesus Christ, Who grants me His life-giving word, making me capable of the Resurrection of Life. O Lord, may Your word be my "final word" today, that my "illness" not be unto death, even in my imperfections. Amen!

FRIDAY, 6ᵗʰ WEEK

TRANSITIONING TO HOLY WEEK

"We have finished the spiritually-beneficial forty days! O Lover of Mankind, we ask: Grant us also to see the Holy Week of Your passion, that we may glorify Your mighty deeds, and Your ineffable dispensation for our sakes, as we sing with one mind: Lord, glory to You!" (Lenten Triodion, Friday of Week 6)

Today is a difficult day to write one of these reflections, because there is so much going on in our liturgical calendar(s). Some of us, on the Older Calendar, are celebrating the great feast of the Annunciation, or "the beginning of our salvation" (as this feast is called in its Troparion-hymn). At the same time, we are transitioning to the beginning of Holy Week, having "finished the forty days" of Lent, according to the Byzantine liturgical calendar. Today Lazarus rests in his tomb for the third day, to be raised from the dead tomorrow by the all-powerful Word of God.

As I am carried into all these mysteries, which unfold before me in our beautiful traditions, I ask in the above-quoted hymn that I be given "to see" the great, "ineffable dispensation for our sakes." Indeed, I need to ask for this vision, lest the hustle-and-bustle of my pre-Paschal preparations distracts me from the Vanquisher of Death, Whom we now prepare to accompany into Jerusalem. Hosanna! Blessed is He Who comes in the name of the Lord!

SATURDAY, 6th WEEK (Resurrection of Lazarus)

THE RESURRECTION OF LAZARUS

"Then Jesus, again greatly disturbed, came to the tomb. It was a cave, and a stone was lying against it. Jesus said, 'Take away the stone.' Martha, the sister of the dead man, said to him, 'Lord, already there is a stench because he has been dead four days.' Jesus said

to her, 'Did I not tell you that if you believed, you would see the glory of God?' So they took away the stone. And Jesus looked upward and said, 'Father, I thank you for having heard me. I knew that you always hear me, but I have said this for the sake of the crowd standing here, so that they may believe that you sent me.' When he had said this, he cried with a loud voice, 'Lazarus, come out!' The dead man came out, his hands and feet bound with strips of cloth, and his face wrapped in a cloth. Jesus said to them, 'Unbind him, and let him go.'" (Jn 11: 38-44)

The resurrection of Lazarus is similar, in some ways, to the resurrection of our Lord Jesus Christ. There was "a cave, and a stone," and a "dead man came out…"

But Lazarus's resurrection was also quite different from our Lord's resurrection, which happened in silence. Lazarus was given new life through the spoken Word of God: Our Lord said, "Take away the stone," and prayed to the Father. And finally, He cried with a loud voice, "Lazarus, come out!"

But none of these words needed to be spoken, in the case of the glorious

Resurrection of the eternal Word of God, our Lord Jesus Christ. Because in the case of the God-Man, the very Source of Life was, indeed, dead in "a cave," and sealed with "a stone,"—but death "could not hold Him" (Acts 2: 24). His very divine essence, as Giver of Life and Vanquisher of Death, overcomes death—in silence. His own, divine essence "speaks" for Him, overcoming death.

So let me depend on Christ's all-powerful, life-giving word a little bit more today, as we enter this Holy Week of His passion and resurrection. He can, and does, "take away the stone" from my heart, regardless of the long-standing "stench" or other obstacles I've accumulated in my less-than-perfect Lent. O Lord, "unbind" me, and let me go, toward the upcoming Holy Week and Pascha. Amen!

PALM SUNDAY

THE LORD'S ENTRY INTO JERUSALEM

"The next day a great crowd who had come to the feast heard that Jesus was coming to Jerusalem. So they took

branches of palm trees and went out to meet him, crying, 'Hosanna! Blessed is he who comes in the name of the Lord, even the King of Israel!' And Jesus found a young donkey and sat upon it; as it is written, 'Fear not, daughter of Zion; behold, your king is coming, sitting on an donkey's colt!' His disciples did not understand this at first; but when Jesus was glorified, then they remembered that this had been written of him and had been done to him. The crowd that had been with him when he called Lazarus out of the tomb and raised him from the dead bore witness. The reason why the crowd went to meet him was that they heard he had done this sign." (Jn 12: 12-18)

Today we similarly carry branches, "re-presenting," or "again making present" to ourselves and to our world, this historical event. Differently, however, from the great crowd in Jerusalem 2,000 years ago (and even Christ's disciples), we understand that we are not greeting an earthly king. Nor do we exclaim, "Hosanna! (Save, we pray!)," expecting from Him deliverance from our earthly or political foes. We greet the Vanquisher of Death, Who today enters Jerusalem to meet His death.

And it is "by death,"—by walking through it—that He will "trample death." This victory will be invisible, very early next Sunday morning.

As we greet our Lord today, carrying branches as "signs of victory" (τῆς νίκης σύμβολα φέροντες, победы знамения носяще), I am reminded to "Fear not, daughter of Zion!" I'm reminded to "fear not" the journey of the Cross, which Christ has come to share with us, and to crown with His kind of victory, not ours. Let me "come" today, in His name, and be blessed. *"Blessed is he who comes in the name of the Lord!"*

Chapter Eight: Great Week & Pascha

HOLY & GREAT MONDAY

BEHOLD, THE BRIDEGROOM

"Behold, the Bridegroom comes at midnight, / And blessed is that servant whom He shall find watching, / And again, unworthy is the servant whom He shall find heedless. / Beware, therefore, O my soul, do not be weighed down with sleep, / Lest you be given up to death, and lest you be shut out of the Kingdom. / But rouse yourself crying: Holy, Holy, Holy, art Thou, O our God, / Through the Theotokos have mercy on us." (Troparion-Hymn of "Bridegroom Matins" on Holy Monday, Tuesday, and Wednesday)

This hymn, chanted in our churches at the morning-service of the first three days of this Holy and Great Week of our Lord's passion, refers to the Parable of the Ten Virgins (Mt 25: 1-13). In that well-known parable, there are five "wise" virgins, signifying those of us who are well-prepared, with "oil" in our "lamps," or with God's mercy and compassion in our hearts, when our "Bridegroom," Jesus Christ, arrives to invite us "in" to His feast. There are also five "foolish" virgins, who, like me, are not thus prepared.

So Jesus is the intended "Bridegroom" of all of us—of the Church. Because what He seeks with each of us is union, or, more specifically, "communion." As St. Paul says about the marital union, *"This is a great mystery, and I am talking about Christ and His Church"* (Eph 5: 32).

Even if I've been "foolish" thus far, let me not be discouraged. Let me be "roused" at this point, opening my heart to God's mercy and compassion, as I am called in this beautiful hymn. My Bridegroom "comes" at the end of this week "at midnight," on the night of His glorious Resurrection, when we will be greeting Him, singing, "Christ is risen from the dead..." As I prepare for Pascha, I depend not on my own prayers or virtues for my "oil," but appeal to one Virgin wiser and more compassionate than all other "wise" virgins, the Mother of God: *"Through the Theotokos have mercy on us."*

HOLY & GREAT TUESDAY

I HAVE NO GARMENT

"I see Your bridal chamber adorned, O my Saviour, and I have not the garment, to enter therein; O Giver of Light, make radiant the vesture of my soul, and save me." (Exaposteilarion-Hymn of "Bridegroom Matins" on Holy Monday, Tuesday, and Wednesday)

Some of us have not fasted enough, or prayed enough, to be well-prepared for the upcoming celebration of Pascha. But in fact the hymns of this Holy and Great Week, like the one quoted above, speak of and for all of us, as ill-prepared for the "bridal chamber" that is the upcoming celebration.—Like the man in the Parable of the Wedding Banquet, who is found to have no "wedding garment," and is thrown out for his impropriety (Mt 22: 1-14).

But today let me let go of any preoccupation with my "ill-preparedness" and join the celebration, handing over "the vesture of my soul" to the Giver of Light. Because I have a Bridegroom Who has overcome my sinful state of affairs by taking them on, having been stripped naked, crucified, and vanquishing all that in His death and resurrection. O Lord, as You head toward Your cross for my sake, please do for me what I can't do for myself: *"Make radiant the vesture of my soul, and save me."*

HOLY & GREAT WEDNESDAY

JUDAS THE "SCROOGE"

"Now when Jesus was at Bethany in the house of Simon the leper, a woman came up to him with an alabaster flask of very expensive ointment, and she poured it on his head, as he sat at table. But when the disciples saw it, they were indignant, saying, 'Why this waste? For this ointment might have been sold for a large sum, and given to the poor.' But Jesus, aware of this, said to them, 'Why do you trouble the woman? For she has done a beautiful thing for me (εἰς ἐμέ). *For you always have the poor with you, but you will not always have me. In pouring this ointment on my body she has done it to prepare me for burial. Truly, I say to you, wherever this gospel is preached in the whole world, what she has done will be told in memory of her.' Then one of the twelve, who was*

called Judas Iscariot, went to the chief priests and said, 'What will you give me if I deliver him to you?' And they paid him thirty pieces of silver. And from that moment he sought an opportunity to betray him." (Mt 26: 6-16)

So the woman who anoints Christ does "a beautiful thing" for Him—personally and concretely for Jesus Christ, in the here and now. And that "here and now" happens to be this week of His passion, when he finds Himself on the outskirts of Jerusalem—a dangerous place because of the chief-priests who, at this point, were seeking to destroy Him. But the concern of "the disciples," which, according to another Gospel (Jn 12: 4-5) is voiced by Judas, is impersonal—for "the (nameless) poor," in their unnamed needs in the uncertain future.

Judas is a miser, which means he views money as something to be hoarded for some future, vaguely identified, need or calamity. It also means he has replaced with money the love and nourishment of a connection with others, including God, like Dickens's "Scrooge." Judas is "nurtured" by possessing money, having become dead to any real connection with

Christ or anyone else. So, he acts alone, and he dies alone, with his "thirty pieces of silver" proving useless to him in the end.

Let me keep watch today, on this Holy and Great Wednesday, that any money I may possess is not, delusionally, "a beautiful thing" for me. A truly "beautiful thing" is to do, with money, what I am called to do in the here and now, according to my vocation. And that means, doing for those in my here and now, whom I have been called to serve and minister to, according to my concrete responsibilities and God-given relationships. For I will always have "the poor" with me, but I may not always have these beloved people in my vicinity.

HOLY & GREAT THURSDAY

A NEW COVENANT

"And when the hour came, he sat at table, and the apostles with him. And he said to them, 'I have earnestly desired to eat this passover with you before I suffer; for I tell you I shall not eat it until it is fulfilled in the kingdom of God.' And he took a cup, and when he

had given thanks he said, 'Take this, and divide it among yourselves; for I tell you that from now on I shall not drink of the fruit of the vine until the kingdom of God comes.' And he took bread, and when he had given thanks he broke it and gave it to them, saying, 'This is my body which is given for you. Do this in remembrance of me.' And likewise the cup after supper, saying, 'This cup which is poured out for you is the new covenant in my blood. But behold the hand of him who betrays me is with me on the table." (Lk 22: 14-20)

"Take this," Jesus says, on this Holy and Great Thursday, "and divide it among yourselves." Because He is, shockingly, entrusting the distribution of His "new covenant," of sacramental communion with His goodness and God-ness, in Body and Blood, to His imperfect followers, the Apostles.—Most of these men, except John, were about to abandon Him at the time of His arrest and crucifixion, in case you didn't know.

But all that—all of our human weakness, was overcome and made OK, by our Lord's death and resurrection, because He "trampled" our human darkness and death, by walking through it Himself. Our "new covenant" or "new connection" with

God and all His goodness is, simply put, Him. In the flesh. In His Body and Blood. He does for us what we never could do for ourselves. I can "do" in Him and with Him what I could never do in and with my own self.

So let me let go of self-reliance and self-preoccupation today, and partake of Him, despite my imperfection. He gives of Himself to my imperfection, by the hands of His imperfect ministers, in this great sacrament He instituted today, of Holy Communion. It is not about us. As I "do this" it is not about me, but rather "in remembrance of Him," lest I forget Who it is, Who accomplishes my salvific, new connection, or "new covenant," with God and all his good creation. So let me communicate today, in and with Him, rather than self-isolate. *"Of Your mystical Supper, O Son of God, accept me today as a communicant!"* (Вечери твоея тайныя днесь, Сыне Божий, причастника мя приими...)

HOLY & GREAT FRIDAY

MY GOD, MY GOD, WHY...?

"And when the sixth hour had come, there was darkness over the whole land

until the ninth hour. And at the ninth hour Jesus cried with a loud voice, 'Elo-i, Elo-i, lama sabachthani?' which means, 'My God, my God, why have you forsaken me?' And some of the bystanders hearing it said, 'Behold, he is calling Elijah.' And one ran and, filling a sponge full of vinegar, put it on a reed and gave it to him to drink, saying, 'Wait, let us see whether Elijah will come to take him down.' And Jesus uttered a loud cry, and breathed his last. And the curtain of the temple was torn in two, from top to bottom. And when the centurion, who stood facing him, saw that he thus breathed his last, he said, 'Truly this man was the Son of God!'" (Mk 15: 33-39)

Centuries before the events of this Holy and Great Friday, when the All-powerful became powerless, and the Life-Giver died, the Prophet Isaiah explained that "we" were the ones "in trouble," and not Him, even while those who had Him crucified believed He was disrupting "our peace." But He took our "trouble" and false "peace" upon Himself, in order to expose it, and vanquish it, in Him: *"He bears our sins,"* Isaiah proclaims, *"and is pained for us: yet we accounted him to be in trouble, and in suffering, and in affliction. But he was wounded on account of our sins, and was bruised because of our iniquities: the chastisement of our peace* (παιδεία εἰρήνης ἡμῶν) *was upon him; and by his wounds we were healed."* (Is 53: 4-5)

As I weep today, with the Church, beholding the crucifixion, abandonment, and death of our Lord many Fridays ago, I remember that He takes all our darkness upon Himself willfully, in order to bring us out of it into new Life and new Light, with Him and in Him. He takes on our derision, anger, cruelty, despair, and injustice—so we no longer need to unleash those things on one another, nor upon ourselves. "For God so loved the world." (Jn 3: 16) Glory be to Him.

HOLY & GREAT SATURDAY

THE SILENCE OF HOLY SATURDAY

"When You did descend to death, O Life Immortal, / You did slay hell with the splendor of Your Godhead, / And when from the depths You did raise the dead, / All the Powers of Heaven cried out, / O Giver of Life, Christ our God, glory to You!" (Troparion Hymn of Holy & Great Saturday)

The great "silence" of Holy Saturday, when the God-Man lies in the tomb, is different for all those involved. For Joseph of Arimathea and the women who had seen "how his body was laid," and now, on the Sabbath, "rested according to the commandment" (Lk 23: 56), it was a day of great mourning and buried hope.

For us, however, today's "silence" is more like the calm before a storm. Because we know that the Lord of the Sabbath is "working" even as "all mortal flesh" is silent in the face of His horrifying death: *"My Father is working still,"* He told us on another Saturday, *"and I am working." (Jn 5: 17)*

And so it is on this Great and Holy Saturday, when the Source of Life descends into death and hell, not as one defeated, but as Victor; as One Whom "death could not hold." (Acts 2: 24) He "slays hell" already today, and brings new life, in Him, to those who were stuck there. This is why our icon of the feast of the Resurrection depicts this day, Holy Saturday, or Christ's victorious descent into Hades. *"O Giver of Life,"* as we anticipate Your exit from the Tomb in the great silence of today, *"Christ our God, glory to You!"*

PASCHA-SUNDAY
(The Resurrection of Our Lord)

WHY DO YOU SEEK THE LIVING AMONG THE DEAD?

"But on the first day of the week, at early dawn, they came to the tomb, taking the spices that they had prepared. They found the stone rolled away from the tomb, but when they went in, they did not find the body. While they were perplexed about this, suddenly two men in dazzling clothes stood beside them. The women were terrified and bowed their faces to the ground, but the men said to them, 'Why do you seek the living among the dead? He is not here, but has risen...'" (Lk 24: 1-6)

The two angels, the "two men in dazzling clothes" are not all that direct in delivering the news of the resurrection. First, they allow the women to be "perplexed" for a bit, about the rolled-away stone. And then "suddenly," the two make their appearance, and introduce themselves with the silliest question: "Why do you seek the living among the dead?"

Now, please excuse me—But what a question! I mean, after all that had happened, of COURSE these heartbroken women sought their crucified and buried Lord "among the dead." After all, they had seen Him breathe His last, and die, and be buried. And then they had spent all of Saturday in deep mourning.

But here's the charming thing about this vital moment in Salvation History: The two angels apparently take delight in delivering the good news of Christ's resurrection to the women in this playful, gradual way: "Why," they first ask, "do you seek the living among the dead?" Only after that, they deliver the good news, and explain: "He is not here, but is risen…"

I have no deep theological point to make here today, except to note the playfulness of our joy today, in our Lord's resurrection. Christ is risen from the dead, so let all the darkness and earnestness of death be trampled, by Him. Christ is risen, dear zillions! So please relax, and enjoy the grace of the feast!

Chapter Nine: Bright Week

BRIGHT MONDAY

HE KNOWS MY NAME

"But Mary stood weeping outside the tomb. As she wept, she bent over to look into the tomb; and she saw two angels in white, sitting where the body of Jesus had been lying, one at the head and the other at the feet. They said to her, 'Woman, why are you weeping?' She said to them, 'They have taken away my Lord, and I do not know where they have laid him.' When she had said this, she turned around and saw Jesus standing there, but she did not know that it was Jesus. Jesus said to her, 'Woman, why are you weeping? Whom are you looking for?' Supposing him to be the gardener, she said to him, 'Sir, if you have carried him away, tell me where you have laid him, and I will take him away.' Jesus said to her, 'Mary!' She turned and said to him in Hebrew, 'Rabbouni!' (which means Teacher)." (Jn 20: 11-16)

Mary Magdalene does not recognize our Lord, nor does she stop weeping, until He says her name: "Mary!"

Because He said it like nobody else. In His divine love and omniscience, the Lord really "knew" her name; He knew, and understood, her entire identity—what and who she was, and what and who she wasn't. So, she takes great consolation in hearing Him call her name.

Today I take great consolation in being "known," understood, and called, as all of us are, by our one-and-only Creator and Teacher. He does not torment me by "not understanding" me. So I can be myself, and let go of any masks I may wear for other, simply-human beings, as I approach Him today, in simple and heartfelt prayer.

"Woman, why are you weeping?" He asks me today, and "Whom are you looking for?" I can stop weeping, and stop looking, because my Teacher is alive and well today, for my sake. Christ is risen from the dead, dear zillions, "and cannot die again" (Rom 6: 9). So let me respond to Him, Who loves and knows me, as I am.

BRIGHT TUESDAY

A NEW DRINK

"Come, let us drink a new drink (Δεῦτε πόμα πίωμεν καινόν, Приидите пиво пием новое), */ not one miraculously brought forth from a barren rock / but the Fountain of Incorruption, / springing forth from the tomb of Christ, // in Whom we are strengthened."* (Paschal Canon, Irmos of Ode 3)

The Lord's resurrection changes things, including our "drinking habits." That is to say, the new Life and new Strength "springing forth from the tomb" is offered to me as a new "Fountain," to which I can come and quench my inner "thirst," or the hole in my heart. It is not merely water "brought forth from a barren rock," as Moses did for his people in the waterless desert (Numbers 20: 11).

We "are strengthened" continuously, on a daily basis, in and through communion with Christ, Who walks with us on our cross-carrying journeys, as One already-victorious, as One Who knows well, and has overcome, the full extent of our darkness and difficulties. So today let me "come," once again, and "drink a new drink," offered to me in abundance in the Self-Offering of my Lord, Who is risen indeed!

BRIGHT WEDNESDAY

HE COULDN'T BE HELD

" 'Men of Israel, hear these words: Jesus of Nazareth, a man attested to you by God with mighty works and wonders and signs which God did through him in your midst, as you yourselves know— this Jesus, delivered up according to the definite plan and foreknowledge of God, you crucified and killed by the hands of lawless men. But God raised him up, having loosed the pangs of death, because it was not possible for him to be held by it.' " (St. Peter's speech on Pentecost, Acts 2: 22-24)

Pentecost is still many weeks away, but I am already called to anticipate it in the above-quoted passage, read in our churches today. Here St. Peter, filled with the Holy Spirit, is "making sense" of Christ's death and resurrection. He offers me the simplest and clearest "explanation" of our Lord's rising up from the dead— "because it was not possible for Him to be held" by death. Divinity, the Source of Life, could not be held by death. Humanity, on the other hand, "could" be held by death, and was, indeed, "held" by it—before humanity's unique union with divinity in the Person of Jesus Christ. When death came up against the God-Man, Who took it on willfully, "according to the definite plan and foreknowledge of God," it was irreparably damaged, losing its "sting" and its "hold" on all who willfully choose to live and die in Christ.

We still die a physical death, but we die differently, just like we live differently, in Christ. The meaning of "death" and "life" is forever changed through Christ's salvific journey through our life and our death. It is now His kind of death, and His kind of life, that we receive, if we willfully walk the cross-carrying journey with Him. But just talking about it, or reading about it, doesn't do me much good. I need to try it today, and once again re-connect with His Spirit, that I may experience this new kind of living and dying, not in lonely isolation, but as one belonging to His light-filled Body. So that I know what it means, not to be "held" by death. Thank You,

Lord, for being One of us, that we may become one, in You.

BRIGHT THURSDAY

SHINE, SHINE!

"Shine, shine (Φωτίζου, φωτίζου, Светися, светися), O New Jerusalem, for the glory of the Lord has risen upon you. Dance now and be glad, O Sion, and you rejoice, pure Mother of God, at the arising of Him to Whom you gave birth." (Paschal Canon, Irmos of Ode 9)

Here are some fun facts about this well-known hymn of our Paschal services. It begins by paraphrasing the words of Isaiah 60: 1, according to the Septuagint: "Shine, shine, O Jerusalem (Φωτίζου, φωτίζου, Ιερουσαλημ)," says Isaiah, "for your light is come, and the glory of the Lord is risen upon you." The hymn is referring these words to the "new" Jerusalem or Sion—the Church—in other words, all of us.

And finally the hymn addresses yet another image of the Church, the Mother of God. She classically signifies the Church, because the Church, i.e., each of us, is called to give birth to the Word of God in this world. So let me do so today, and let me "shine," as I am called to, with and in my risen Lord. Because "my light is come," as prophesied by Isaiah, and He is risen indeed!

BRIGHT FRIDAY

THOSE IN THE TOMBS (СУЩИЕ ВО ГРОБЕХ)

"Christ is risen from the dead, / trampling down death by death, / and upon those in the tombs (καὶ τοῖς ἐν τοῖς μνήμασι, и сущим во гробех) */ bestowing life!"* (Byzantine Troparion-hamn of Pascha/Easter)

So—who are "those in the tombs"? All of us, practically. "Those in the tombs" are those of us "buried," either in our work or in a relationship, or in a "dead" indifference to work or a relationship (I realize that sounds paradoxical, but both those situations are "deadening"); or in some obsession or addiction, like an unhealthy dependency on a thing or person.

But Christ "is risen" from all our darkness, having walked through it;

having confronted all our weakness, anger, resentment, fear, despondency, and insufficiency, which led Him to the Cross—which was His calling or "vocation." He "trampled" all our "death" and deadness, by walking through that "death," and rising from it, as He was "called" to do by the Father, and as only He could, as the Source of Life, in His divinity.

So I can also walk through it all today, but not on my own. I can trample death "by death," by walking in and with Him through my vocation and responsibilities, which may, at times, —when I try to tackle them on my own—seem dark and deadening. But, paradoxically, they (my vocation and responsibilities) are also the very thing that leads me to life, because I am called to do them. And Christ has paved the way for me, which is the way of the Cross, of not avoiding my responsibilities, but walking through them, in and with Him. So let me receive life, by walking through it, because it is "bestowed" to me by One Who knows the way out of my "tomb," which is, paradoxically, my vocation. So let me take it up today, handing it over to Him in heartfelt prayer, and opening up to His help. *"Christ is risen from the dead,"* dear zillions, *"trampling down death by death, and upon those in the tombs bestowing life!"*

BRIGHT SATURDAY

THE BREAD OF LIFE

"Jesus said to them, 'I am the bread of life (ὁ ἄρτος τῆς ζωῆς); *he who comes to me shall not hunger, and he who believes in me shall never thirst. But I said to you that you have seen me and yet do not believe. All that the Father gives me will come to me; and him who comes to me I will not cast out..."* (Jn 6: 35-37)

Today, on Bright Saturday, the special Easter "Bread" or "Artos," which we see on a small table before the iconostasis in our churches all of Bright Week, is broken and distributed to the faithful. The "Artos" was first blessed on the night of Pascha, and carried around the church in processions throughout this week. It signifies, or points to, the presence of the Lord among us, His disciples, after His resurrection.

So that is why I'm thinking about this passage, in which Christ calls Himself "the bread of life." Here He also says to the crowd, nay, pleads with the crowd, to believe Him. "You have seen me and yet do not believe." Because He knows we are a disbelieving bunch, with "trust issues" when it comes to Him. Nonetheless, if you "come to me," however and whoever you are, He assures me, I will not cast you out.

And tomorrow, on Thomas Sunday, He will further address our doubts, and further assure us, also those of us who did not see Him in the flesh as those first disciples did: "Blessed are those who have not seen," He will say to all of us, "and yet have believed." (Jn 20: 29) So today "Do not be faithless, but believe" (Jn 20: 27), I hear Him say to me, because I have that choice. I can, indeed, approach Him, the Bread of Life, once again. And once again, I will not hunger, or thirst, or, indeed, be "cast out," for He is risen indeed!

ABOUT THE AUTHOR

Dr. Sr. Vassa Larin, host of the popular, online program, "Coffee with Sister Vassa," is a scholar of Byzantine Liturgy and author of many publications, both scholarly and popular, on Eastern Orthodox spirituality and tradition. Born in Nyack, New York in a devout, Russian Orthodox family, Sister Vassa is now based in Vienna, Austria.

For more on her internationally-acclaimed, online ministry, visit **coffeewithsistervassa.com.**

Books by Sister Vassa Larin:

Lent with Sister Vassa: Reflections for every day of Lent

HealthyFast Lenten Guidebook: Reflections and Meal Plans for Every Day of Lent

Reflections with Morning Coffee: 365 Daily Devotions for Busy People

Tune in to Sr. Vassa's weekly audio-podcasts!

Inspiring & informative topics like

- Making Scripture Part of Your Life;
- Making Decisions & Anxiety;
- Great Feasts of the Church Year
- The 'Crowning' Rite of Marriage;
- The Ageing Process in Faith....
  and much more!

Subscribe here to join our zillions of happy listeners:

patreon.com/sistervassa

www.ingramcontent.com/pod-product-compliance
Lightning Source LLC
Chambersburg PA
CBHW052108110526
44592CB00013B/1526